Scavengers

Jeanne Sturm

Rourke
Educational Media

rourkeeducationalmedia.com

www.rourkeeducationalmedia.com

PHOTO CREDITS: Cover: © Villiers Steyn; Title Page: © Bernhard Richter; 2: © Certifiable; Page 4: © Danin Tulic, FabioFilzi; Page 6: © MrSegui, ray roper, Paul Tessier; Page 7: © Peter Miller, Vadim Ledyaev; Page 8: © Johannes Gerhardus Swanepoel; Page 9: © Anna Bryukhanova; Page 10: © Mirceax; Page 11: © Lucian Coman; Page 12: © Smellme; Page 13: © William Davies; Page 14: © Rob Thoma, Kclarksphotography; Page 15: © Marion Wear, Stacy Barnett; Page 16: © arlindo71, marcus jones, arlindo71; Page 17: © R_R, marcus jones; Page 18: © Willtu; Page 19: © Hinnamsaisuy, Devonyu; Page 20: © Smellme, Photomyeye, Kclarksphotography, Kwiktor, Jeffrey Skopin, HansUntch, jonesmarc; Page 21: © Bernhard Richter, enviromantic, Ryan Lane, Christian Rummel, Sadi Ugur OKÇu, Andrejs Jegorovs, Photodisc, Mazikab, Peter Malsbury, Georg Hanf, Doug Hudson; Page 22: © Fotoeye75;

Edited by Precious McKenzie

Cover Design by Renee Brady
Interior Design by Cory Davis

Library of Congress PCN Data

Scavengers / Jeanne Sturm
(Eye to Eye with Animals)
ISBN 978-1-61810-116-7 (hard cover) (alk. paper)
ISBN 978-1-61810-249-2 (soft cover)
Library of Congress Control Number: 2011944407

Rourke Educational Media
Printed in the United States of America,
North Mankato, Minnesota

Educational Media

rourkeeducationalmedia.com

customerservice@rourkeeducationalmedia.com • PO Box 643328 Vero Beach, Florida 32964

Table of Contents

Chapter 1
Carrion Eaters

Have you ever seen a large group of vultures gathered by the side of the road, pecking away at something? You can't tell what it is, but as you get closer, and the birds scatter, you can finally see what is holding their interest. An animal has died and the vultures are making a meal of its remains.

Griffon Vulture

Vultures are scavengers. They do not hunt and kill their own food. Instead, they eat **carrion**, meat from animals that are already dead and decaying. Sounds pretty gross, doesn't it? But scavengers perform a very important service to the ecosystem. They clean up what could otherwise become a huge, smelly mess!

Chapter 2

Vultures: Nature's Winged Recyclers

Turkey vultures and black vultures inhabit areas of North America and all of South America. Turkey vultures eat carrion, including dead squirrels, mice, rabbits, birds, reptiles, and skunks. They fill out their diet with leaves, grass, and seeds.

Turkey Vulture

Black Vulture

Vultures and Hyena

▲ *Vultures, jackals, and hyenas eat carrion. Raccoons and opossums consume their share of dead meat, but they also eat fruits, vegetables, bird eggs, and insects.*

Where in the world do vultures live?

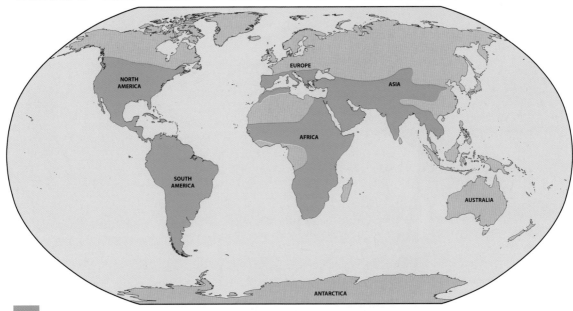

■ *Vulture Habitat Area*

▲ *Vultures live in North America, South America, Europe, Asia, and Africa.*

Vultures have adapted to their diet of rotting meat. When they eat, they stick their heads into the **carcasses** of dead animals. If their heads were feathered, pieces of meat would stick to them and become a smelly, rotten mess. Instead, vultures have bald heads that stay cleaner when they eat.

Why doesn't a vulture become sick from eating rotten meat? The answer lies in its digestive system. Acids in the vulture's stomach kill any bacteria or disease that was present in their meal.

Vultures spend their flight time searching for food. From thousands of feet in the air, they look for their next meal. They don't waste energy flying to such heights. Instead, they catch a ride on a thermal, a column of warm air rising from the ground, and glide through the sky. Turkey vultures, with their keen sense of smell, also fly closer to the ground in order to sniff out decaying meat.

Vultures lay their eggs on the ground, in the hollow of a fallen tree, or in a cave. Turkey vultures raise one **brood** a year, laying from one to three eggs at a time. After their babies hatch, both mother and father share responsibility for their feeding.

▲ *You won't find worms in these babies' diets! Vultures start their babies off with partly digested carrion. Mother and father feed on dead animals, then return to the nest to regurgitate the meal into their babies' mouths. As the babies get older, the parents cough up undigested meat.*

Chapter 3
Scavengers Everywhere

Hyenas live on the dry scrubland and rocky brush of Africa and Asia. Spotted hyenas are skilled hunters, often working in groups to bring down large prey. They are also scavengers and, in large groups, will drive a lion off its prey.

Hyenas have powerful jaws. They can tear apart, eat, and digest parts of animals that other carnivores cannot, including skin and bone. Hyenas are unable to digest some parts, though, including hooves, hair, and **ligaments**. Instead, they **regurgitate** these parts as pellets.

Opossums eat a variety of foods. As scavengers, they make meals of dead animals, often finding carrion alongside the road. Trash cans and dumpsters also provide easy pickings. In the wild, opossums **supplement** their diet of mice, birds, snakes, and insects with grasses, nuts, and fruit.

Opossums face threats from predators, including cats, dogs, foxes, and owls. They face habitat loss when humans cut down forests to make way for farms and neighborhoods. Ironically, a third threat comes just when an opossum thinks it has made a lucky find. While it dines on a dead animal lying by the side of the road, eating the **roadkill** puts the scavenger at the same risk of being hit and killed by a passing car.

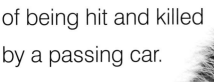

Playing Possum

When an opossum feels threatened, it curls up on its side and plays dead. It can lie still for up to 6 hours, eyes and mouth open, waiting for its predators to lose interest and walk away. Sometimes it gives off a foul odor for added effect.

Cockroaches have lived on Earth for over 340 million years. Most cockroach **species** live in the woods and dine on dead plants. Others eat dead animal and plant material. American and German cockroaches are attracted to warm, moist places.

▶▶
The scent of food and waste attracts cockroaches into homes, where they feast on food scraps, decaying plant and animal matter, and even leather, glue, and hair.

17

Chapter 4
Recyclers of the Water World

The ocean has its share of scavengers, including some sharks that use their keen sense of smell to locate dead animals. Great white sharks, usually solitary animals, sometimes gather in pairs or in small groups to **consume** a carcass. Larger sharks eat first; everyone else gets the leftovers.

Great White Shark

Most crabs are scavengers. As decaying plants and the bodies of dead animals fall to the ocean floor, crabs are there to grab them with their strong claws and tear them into bite-sized pieces.

Blue Crab

Crabs live throughout Earth's oceans, from the cold polar waters to the tropics. Some species live in lakes and rivers, making their homes in rocks or mud. ▶▶

Chapter 5

Thank You, Scavengers!

Scavengers are important links in the **food chain**. Not only do they clean up the messy remains of dead animals, they are also part of the cycle that returns nutrients to the soil.

Vulture

Hyena

Jackal

Opossum

Raccoon

Cockroach

Shark

Crab

Food Chain

Producers
trees, grass, and plants

Primary consumers
zebra, elephant

Secondary consumers
cheetah, lion

Scavengers
vulture, hyena

Decomposers
mushrooms, insects, microorganisms

Scavengers help keep Earth clean by eating food that would make the rest of us sick. They work together with **decomposers** to return nutrients to the soil so new plants can grow. Scavengers are nature's recyclers.

Glossary

brood (brood): a family of young, usually referring to birds

carcasses (KAR-kuhss-uz): animal bodies

carrion (KAIR-ee-uhn): meat from dead animals

consume (kuhn-SOOM): to eat

decomposers (dee-kuhm-PO-zuhrs): bacteria and fungi that break down organic waste and dead organisms

food chain (food chayn): ordered series of animals and plants in which each feeds on the one below it

ligaments (LIG-uh-muhnts): strong bands of tissue that hold bones together at a joint

regurgitate (ree-GUR-juh-tate): to return food that has been swallowed back to the mouth

roadkill (ROHD-kil): an animal that has been struck and killed by a passing car

species (SPEE-sheez): a group of living things so similar to one another they can mate and produce offspring

supplement (suhp-luh-muhnt): to make up for something that is missing

Index

Websites To Visit

www.nhptv.org/natureworks/nwep11.htm

www.fcps.edu/islandcreekes/ecology/turkey_vulture.htm

www.sandiegozoo.org/animalbytes/t-striped_hyena.html

About the Author

Jeanne Sturm lives in Florida with her husband, Kurt, and children, David, Krista, and Robert. She enjoys reading, bicycling, and windsurfing. Although scavengers aren't her favorite animals, she does enjoy spotting wildlife while hiking and bicycling in the conservation area near her home.

Ask The Author!
www.rem4students.com